Anonymous

An Answer to the Anonymous Remarks on a Letter From

Warren Hastings, Esq.,

to the Court of Directors

Anonymous

An Answer to the Anonymous Remarks on a Letter From Warren Hastings, Esq.,
to the Court of Directors

ISBN/EAN: 9783337012540

Printed in Europe, USA, Canada, Australia, Japan

Cover: Foto ©Suzi / pixelio.de

More available books at **www.hansebooks.com**

AN

ANSWER

TO THE

ANONYMOUS REMARKS

ON A

LETTER

FROM

WARREN HASTINGS, Esq.

TO THE

COURT of DIRECTORS.

─────────

LONDON:

PRINTED FOR JOHN STOCKDALE,
OPPOSITE BURLINGTON-HOUSE, PICCADILLY.
M.DCC.LXXXVI.

[Price ONE SHILLING.]

AN

ANSWER, &c.

A Letter dated fo long ago as 21ft February, 1784, from Mr. Haftings to the Court of Directors, now firft exhibited to the world in form of a pamphlet, and made a vehicle for the introduction of illiberal reflections, and anonymous remarks, affords a ftrong prefumption of the laboratory where the pitiful compofition was fabricated. Internal evidence corroborates the fufpicion. Much and accurate local knowledge joined with deliberate mifreprefentation, and unfupported affertions delivered with a farcaftic flippancy of ftyle, form a character fo legible, that it is impoffible to doubt the hand.—The judicious choice of *time* for this publication throws additional light on the conjecture: for, even the temper of

the

the Houfe of Commons may be affected by a momentary delufion ; and the fophiftry of thefe *Remarks* may have worked its intended operation before Mr. Haftings or his friends can have had leifure to refute it.

The effect which this pamphlet may produce on the deliberations of the Court of Directors, though the oftenfible plea of the writer is certainly but a fecondary (if any) confideration. The Directors have long been in poffeffion of the original letter—Even the remarks are probably no novelty to them. The remarker will not be fufpected of having been able to make fo long a facrifice of his vanity, although in favour of his malice, as to have hitherto fuppreffed the triumphant utterance of them from his own mouth whenever he could hope to lie undetected, or where he knew *fuch* lies would be applauded. He may quote Horace *fui juris*; but the " *nonum prematur in annum*" is not compatible with the thoufandth part of his felf-conceit.

The attention of the public has been fo long directed to the conduct of Mr. Haftings, that it is impoffible the great outlines of his character fhould be now mifunderftood. When, therefore, any picture is drawn, or any feature exhibited with refpect to him, not conformable to thefe out-

no

lines, men are no longer to be blinded by infidious colouring, or mifled by unrefembling caricature.

Sufpicions have been fo often fomented, and fo fully difpelled.—Prejudices have been fo artfully raifed, and fo completely counteracted, that of all the tales induftrioufly circulated to his difadvantage, not one has lived long enough to anfwer the purpofe of the inventor.—Four lines quoted from the very letter in queftion, will abundantly fatisfy all the *impartial* and *candid* part of my readers on the prefent topic. It is Mr. Haftings that fpeaks—and they are now in the habit of believing *him.*————

" Improvident, (fays he) for myfelf, zealous for the " honour of my country, and the credit and interefts of my " employers, I feldom permitted my profpects of futurity " to enter into the views of my private concerns."——

Is it extraordinary, that a man who has done fo much good, and refifted fo much evil, who has for twelve years fupported the powers of his government, and the very exiftence of the Britifh nation in India, againft all the enemies of his country, and the oppofition of almoft all his affociates, fhould have had little time to think of his own concerns?—Is it wonderful that a man, who is confeffedly

improvident

improvident fhould not be *rich?* The very *articles* charged in the account annexed to his letter are themfelves a full proof of the exiftence and extent of that improvidence.

For above twelve years together he fuffers charges clearly of a *public* nature, to be carried to the account of his own *private expence.*— He fuffers this, I fay, *unconcerned,* when he might have feized a thoufand opportunities of momentary influence in Council, during that period, to have paffed every item of them at the *Board of Infpection,* which I defy the *Remarker* himfelf to affert, not to have been competent to the purpofe.

The Examiner goes at large into the time and circumftances in which this letter was written. He fcrutinizes each head of the account in all its points of view : he enters into the detail of Mr. Haftings's domeftic œconomy in Bengal, with an intimacy not to be acquired at a diftance, —and even defcends to the laborious minutenefs of verbal criticifm. It is to be wifhed, that in his own arrangements there was more perfpicuity, more connexion in his fentences, and more candour as well as more folidity in his obfervations. To remarks fo tautologous and fo diffufe, it is impoffible to give a fimple and compact anfwer.—When an article is confuted on the inftant of its appearance, it ftarts up again at a diftance, in another form ; and, when

one

one page of abufe is gone through, the next exhihits the fame abufe in a different drefs. His arguments are fo verfatile and unfubftantial that they elude the grafp, or vanifh from the touch of vigorous examination; and the pitiful fhadow, of a jeft * muft occafionally fupply the place of fober reafoning.

Let us follow the plan (if, in fo vague a performance, any plan can be difcerned or fufpected) of the Remarker. —At leaft, let us firft confider (as he affects to do) the time and circumftances in which Mr. Haftings wrote his letter.—" He knew (fays our *Philippic* page 12) that " the power which had hitherto fupported him, had been " obliged to give away; and that a fyftem from " which he had no protection to expect, was likely to prevail at home"—Alluding to Mr. *Fox*'s entrance into office. Will he then pretend to affert that either of the for- mer adminiftrations—thofe of Rockingham and Shel- burne, were favourable to Mr Haftings? In the firft, Mr. Fox himfelf bore a confiderable fway, and the *grand accufer, l'Avocat mème du diable*, was faftened to the very ear of authority: Lord Shelburne's party, though lefs violent, was not more friendly. And if fear could make any impreffion on Mr. Hafting's mind, it cer- tainly was not a fear of the coalition adminiftration.—But

" private

* See " *moonfbine.*" page 24.

" private letters mention, that when he fet out on his
" laft expedition to Lucknow, his fpirits were funk into
" the loweft ftate of dejection."—Be it fo,—we grant
the fact, and will confider whence it arifes.

Let us now figure to ourfelves the Governor-General,
juft departed from the Seat of Government on an affair
of the firft political confequence, with a conftitution de-
bilitated by long and laborious exertions under an inhof-
pitable climate. He left the Prefidency with a fever
hanging on him. In fome of the folitary hours of a
tedious voyage againft the current of a mighty river
He turns his thoughts for the firft time to a contemplation
of his own private concerns.—He had no reafon to *hope*
that his return to Calcutta would be fpeedy, for the at-
tainment of his object was neceffarily accompanied with
delay: that he could not *fear* a fudden return may be
fairly inferred from his having ventured to embark on fo
delicate an expedition, burthened with fuch a weight of
refponfibility.—but he might perifh in the courfe of it: and
every man who can eftimate the defpondency inevitably
incident to all diforders of the bile, and who can feel
the fad anxiety of having made no preparations for miti-
gating to the furvivor the dreadful diffolution of the ten-
dereft of all connexions, will be amply fatisfied as to the
caufes of Mr. Haftings's uneafinefs.

Domeftic

Domeftic circumftances, in fhort, both authorize and account for his dejection of fpirits. But were public motives only to be allowed on this occafion, they may be imagined both of number and weight fufficient to warrant any degree of diffatisfaction, without giving place among them to apprehenfion for the poffible manœuvres of a " *moonfhine* " Miniftry.—Grofs mifreprefentation at home, and rancorous oppofition abroad.—Parliament and the Public equally hood-winked and deceived—One adminiftration after another bent to entangle, to perplex, and to miftake the affairs of India; or to turn the management of a mighty empire into a pitiful jobb— the anarchy which the very expectation of Mr. Fox's bill produced in Bengal; the confufion and ruin which muft have enfued on its introduction—thefe and a thoufand other political concerns, remote *toto cælo* from all perfonal dread, might allowably fill up the meafure of his defpondency.—And, if the glory of having contributed to the fplendour of the Britifh name, by the eftablifh- ment of its influence and the well-ordering of its govern- ments in India were ever dear to his ambition.——well might he bleed for the threatened execution of meafures fo pernicious and fo deftructive to both. "If his prefent letter,', therefore, " when written, had very much the air of

B   " a wind-

" a winding up, not only of his Government, but of his
" life"—it is not neceſſarily indicative of " *a ſtate of mind*
" *enfeebled and perplexed by the conſciouſneſs of guilt.*" It be-
longs only to men of the Remarker's ſtamp to connect the
ideas of *a laſt dying ſpeech and confeſſion* with the cloſe of
departing exiſtence.—Mr. Haſtings's was the manly me-
lancholy of a *Patriot*, perhaps in ſome degree of a *Huſband,*
but certainly not the cowardly timidity of a Culprit.

" Carrying, therefore, this view of his ſituation and
" reflections into the examination of his letter, we may
" fairly account for many things," (*and for every thing*),
" which he has left unexplained."

On the 22d of May 1782 Mr Haſtings had firſt drawn
up a ſtatement of various ſums of money, applied by his
means to public uſes.—In a ſecond and explanatory letter
of the 16th of December of the ſame year, he writes " the
" ſources from which theſe reliefs to the public ſervice
" have come, would never have yielded them to the com-
" pany *publicly.*"

. . The Court of Directors, in a letter to Bengal, dated
March 16, 1784, thus write, para. 47. " Although it
" is

" is not our intention to *exprefs any doubt of the integrity of*
" *our* Governor-General, on the contrary, after having
" received the prefents, we cannot avoid *expreffing our*
" *approbation of his conduct*, in bringing them to the credit
" of the Company; yet, we muft confefs, the ftatement of
" thofe tranfactions appears to us in many parts fo unin-
" telligible, that we feel ourfelves under the neceffity of
" calling on the Governo-General for an expla-
" nation, &c."

Mr. Haftings arrived in England in June 1785, and
early in July he anfwers fully and fairly this interrogatory,
(though not called upon publicly fo to do) by a letter to
the Chairman, in which he meets the demand in every
ftage, and replies to it: and ftill further refers him " for a
" more minute information, and for the means of making
" any inveftigation which they (the Directors) may think
" it proper to direct—to Mr. Larkins, *who was privy to*
" *every procefs of it*, &c. &c." That is, he has at once put
it out of his own power to glofs over or accommodate to
any future emergency his account of prefents received,
by giving up the perfon in poffeffion of the fums, dates,
names, and every other document neceffary to elucidate the
particulars of thefe tranfactions.

Is this " *an artifice to deceive the multitude?*" is this " *an* " *indication of a mind enfeebled and perplexed by the confciouf-* " *nefs of guilt?* Bengal, though in the uninterrupted enjoyment of wealth, peace, and abundance during the whole period of Mr. Haftings's Government, was at particular moments greatly in want of ready money for the inftant neceffities of a burthenfome war. Mr. Haftings, by his influence as Governor, by his character as a man, or by his connections in confequence of near 30 years refidence, was enabled from time to time to procure fome unexpected affiftance, fome irregular act of benevolence, for the purpofe of a fudden emergency. " The exi- " gences of the Government (fays he) were at that " time my own, and every preffure upon it refted with " its full weight upon my mind. Wherever I could find " allowable means of relieving thofe wants, I eagerly feized " them."——That is, through a fecret and unfufpected channel he derived thef unds for fitting out a military expedition, or anfwering a clamorous demand—to which the public treafury was for the moment unequal: and now we are to be told " it refts with Mr. Haftings or his " friends to fhew what poffible motive, but a corrupt " one, could engage any native to give him money pri- " vately."

From

From the *motive* which might weigh with a native in affifting the ftate through the hands of its ruler, the Remarker paffes to Mr. Haftings's motive in accepting it.

" Receiving money *againft law*, (fays he) is not an in-
" different action in a Governor. If he had no *wrong*
" motive, what motive had he ?—and what was the view
" or expectation of the perfon who gave it?"—We will
anfwer each of thefe points diftinctly.

I. The Law, taken compendioufly, ftates, that all money received by a company's fervant is, bonâ fide, the property of the company—and may be fued for, &c. &c. Mr. Haftings receives money, and makes over the money fo received to the company.—Therefore the law is obferved. —Therefore it is not againft law.

He acknowledges the amount, and gives up the nam^e of the perfon who kept his accounts—Can this with juftice, with decency, with probability, be called "a confeffion which " fpecifies no particulars ?" Much lefs is there any room for the dirty infinuation (page 22) that " in a truft of the " loweft order, fuch a conduct would be deemed fufficient " evidence of fraud."

II. " If

II. "If Mr. Haſtings had no *wrong* motive, what motive had he?"——

——A *right* one. The *raiſon d'etat* in a good ſenſe. A principle of patriotiſm.—To relieve the exigencies of the ſtate by every little aid which "*he could thus Procure*" from ſources "*which would never have yielded them to the Company publicly*"——and why?——becauſe there would have been a reaſonable apprehenſion (as was really the caſe with Cheyt Sing) that a *public* contribution would have furniſhed a dangerous precedent to the Company for claiming a perpetual increaſe of revenue.——In a *private* aid this danger did not exiſt.

III. What then was the *motive* of the *donor?*

——The generoſity of a friend, the ſubtlety of a courtier, the ſervility of an Aſiatic—views of intereſt—hope of favour—dread of neglect—many or all of theſe combined (whether good or bad) might have had their weight. The queſtion is not ſo much what the donor *might* expect, as what *did* the Governor grant. Was Mr. Haſtings a *collector*, that " a " Zemindar ſhould give *him* one lack of rupees, to be " excuſed two in his rent?" The inſtances of ſuch proſtituted and fraudulent patronage (if any exiſted), muſt have been ſufficiently conſpicuous. What Zemindar's rent

rent *could* Mr. Haſtings excuſe or mitigate at pleaſure ?—
The "*meaneſt*" of his colleagues had in that reſpeƈt always
an equal voice ; and, if *He* knows of any ſuch inſtance,
why does he ſhrink from its diſcovery under the cowardly
diſguiſe of *general inſinuation ?* Sifting for private ſcan-
dal from the diſappointed reſentments and unſatisfied ex-
peƈtations of the tenants of Government, is an employment
better ſuited to *ſome* tempers and talents than a liberal en-
quiry into the advantages or celebrity of a Mahommedan
academy. That Mr. Haſtings made *ſome* uſe of his
influence to procure money privately for the ſervice of the
ſtate is allowed.—That he ſacrificed the credit of his
ſtation or the intereſts of his employers, or the integrity
of his principles, in any of theſe inſtances, is utterly de-
nied—and let the inſinuator prove ;

Probatio ſequitur affirmativum.

Of the money acknowledged by Mr. Haſtings to have
paſſed to the Company's account through his hands, a
part is afterwards appropriated to the liquidation of his
own demands upon them.—The Remarker, by his hints,
that the " claim might be ſubjeƈt to difficulties, if really
" left to the Court of Direƈtors ;" and in another place,
that, " ſuppoſing theſe claims of his to be ſuch
" as the Direƈtors are at liberty to deny, if they think
" proper ;"

" proper :"—and by other such pitiful subterfuges, would imprefs an idea which he dares not openly maintain, that these demands are disputable, are injurious, are unjust.— We shall presently have occasion to meet him on this ground :—and in the mean time will suppose the demands to be justified, that we may come to the *mode adopted for payment*. The account is *debited* under the head of " Dur-" bar Charges ;"—which are (as the Remarker states) " an " account of bounties and presents made by Government, " and of secret services only known to the Governor."—— That is, in short, sundry charges incidental to the Go-vernment in the person of the Governor. The *credit* side of this account is an entry of various petty sums received on account of Government from persons mak-ing complimentary visits, &c. to the Governor.—" *Mo-" ney received privately by Mr. Haftings*" could not be entered with propriety under any other head of account. For when some of the money so received was transmitted by * Mr. Haftings at once to the Treafury; he was obliged to enter it as *lent on bond*, or *placed in deposit*, to obviate the curiosity or misapprehensions of the clerks, and to accommodate it to the *official heads of entry in the Company's Books*. Here then is a clue to all the mysteries discovered by the Remarker in Mr. Haftings's letter on

* See his Letter to Mr. Devaynes, dated July 11, 1785.

this

this fubject :—" a fubject (he fays) that demanded nothing
" but plain language, yet the expreffions he (Mr. Haft-
" ings) makes ufe of are for the moft part *affected* and *intri-*
" *cate*, and in fome places *unintelligible*." The money
which Mr. Haftings received privately on the public
account, and expended in *fecret* (or any) fervices for the
public, is entered and paffed in the account of *Durbar
Charges*. The money which, when offered privately, he
never received at all, but transferred at once to the
Company's Treafury, is entered under fome one of the
only heads in the Treafury-books to which it could poffi-
bly be referred—" bonds," or " depofite money," " Thefe
" bonds (fays the Remarker) fuppofing it poffible to
" invent a pretence for this courfe of proceeding - - - - -
" ought to have been cancelled long ago, *which it*
" *is not known that he has done,*" The Remarker has
read, for he has quoted a partial extract in his Appen-
dix from, Mr. Haftings's letter to Mr. Devaynes, of the
11th of July, 1785, which contains the following para-
graph.

" It being my wifh to clear up every doubt upon this
" tranfaction, which either my own mind could fuggeft,
" or which may have been fuggefted by others, I beg
" leave to fuppofe another queftion, and to ftate the terms

C   " of

" cf it in my reply; by informing you that the *indorfement* " *on the bonds was made* about the period of my leaving " the Prefidency, in the middle of the year 1781, *in order* " *to guard againft their becoming a claim on the Company*, as " *part of my eftate, in the event of my death, &c,*" Every man of honour will *here at leaft* difcern the fallacy, and re- probate the malice of the Remarker's argument—who has taken advantage of the omiffion of the formal word "*cancel*", to infinuate that the Bonds are ftill in force—as if an In- dorfement on a Bond, for the exprefs purpofe of *annihila- ting the poffibility of its becoming a claim*, can, in the nature of things, be any thing elfe than a *cancelling !* A Newgate Solicitor would fpurn at fuch a fubterfuge !

To the head of " Durbar Charges" Mr. Haftings places his own demands on the Company: and under the fame head he credits them for a fum of money adequate to the charge, which had come privately into his hands,— " *from a fource which would never have yielded it publicly.*" The Company therefore are not faddled with any addi- tional expence on account of Mr. Haftings's Durbar charges, as the payment of them is not drawn from any part of the Company's annual or ordinary revenue. To this *mode* alfo of payment the Remarker objects, and with his ufual accuracy. See page 23. Is it not true that

I   Bengal

Bengal has " enjoyed the *funfhine* of peace and abun-
" dance" during Mr. Haftings's government;—why then
cavil at the expreffion?—Why are we to " *conclude that*
" *their affairs are in extreme diftrefs*", becaufe out of many
modes that might prefent themfelves for the difcharge of
a debt, Mr. Haftings chofe that which was in itfelf the
fimpleft of all others; and which happened alfo to be
" *the moft fuitable to the Company's affairs?*" It might well
be the *moft fuitable*, becaufe the current revenue was certainly appropriated to fpecific ufes, and abforbed by previous deftinations, from whence it could not be alienated.
Are we neceffarily to conclude that England is on the
verge of ruin, becaufe the Minifter cannot alter the defti-
nation of only 50,000l. to a plan of fortifications, out of
an annual appropriated revenue of 15 millions ? The fum
applied by Mr. Haftings to the account in queftion was
unembarraffed by any previous engagement, and therefore
indifputably moft at liberty to anfwer a new or occafional
demand. So much for the *mode of payment*—we come
now to the *juftnefs of the demand itfelf.*—It confifts of fundry
difburfements made by Mr. Haftings, and ftated to be on
the public account, comprifed under five abftract heads.
See the roth page of the Pamphlet.

1. Salary to Colonel Ironfide, a Military Secretary.

When

When Mr. Haftings firft acceded to the government in 1772, among a thoufand tafks of the moft arduous political nature, a thorough reform in both the civil and military departments was not the leaft of his labours. The *weight*, therefore, as well as the *experience* of a *field-officer*, might be neceffary to correct, to affift, and to execute his plans. But a field-officer might not be inclined, and could not be compelled to ferve in a ftation ufually allotted to inferior rank : or he might at leaft, with decency, ftipulate for an allowance proportionate to his fuperiority. The comparifon of the regular routine of the Britifh ftaff will by no means hold with that of the novel and fluctuating inftitutions of the Bengal army of that period. Mr. Haftings, in his explanatory Letter of the 21ft of February 1784, particularly ftates this temporary addition of falary to have been referred to the Court of Directors, and *no anfwer to have been obtained.* The filence of fuperiors in all fuch cafes of reference muft inevitably pafs for *acquiefcence.* This demand is therefore perfectly *juft.* It is abfurd to fay, that " Colonel Ironfide, as Military Secre-
" tary, had no claim to extraordinary pay from the Com-
" pany, on account of his fuperior rank, *nor does it appear*
" *that he made any.*" He actually *received* extraordinary pay, and therefore the prefumption is, that he *did* claim it. The reference to the Directors was made in " one of the
" general

" general Letters of the year 1773 or 1774:" therefore it
was made with the cognizance and concurrence of the
Board at Calcutta : so that the Remarker's observation in
page 24 does not apply to this article.

2. Charges in the Governor-General's office for twelve
years.

I must here make two remarks upon the 10th page of
the Pamphlet now before me. The first concerns the
article No. 2, in which, by a mistake not noticed among
the *scrupulous* errata at the end, 1774 is put for 1784.
This has the effect of exhibiting the charges accumulated
in above *eleven years*, as the wasteful extravagance of about
sixteen months; and the probability of a typical error re-
serves a plausible retreat for the Remarker's malice. My
next remark is, that, in the note at the bottom of the same
page, (in reference to this article) " *pens, ink, paper*,
tape, &c. are officiously promoted to the foremost place,
while the weighty charges of salaries to clerks, are left to
the last. This may naturally be imputed to a desire of
exciting the Reader's astonishment, by the contrast be-
tween the enormity of the sum and the relative cheapness
of the goods.——Lord North's *Treasury whipcord* is a fool
to it.

Confidering the multiplied functions of the Governor-General's duty, and the very unequal fhare of public bufi-nefs which always refted upon him, (for proof of which I appeal to the Bengal Confultations for any year) an al-lowance of 1100 rupees a month, the average amount of the fum here charged, for a feparate office, is fuch as the moft rigid parfimony could not wifh to curtail. Mr. Haftings's *private affairs* occupied little or no part of this eftablifhment: but a very confiderable fhare was un-doubtedly allotted to his *correfpondence*; any part of which I much wonder the Remarker fhould denominate "*private*," when he fo well knows how often Mr. Haftings has been required and obliged to give it up in detail to *public in-fpection*. The Minifter at home expected and received from the Governor-General a regular and accurate difplay. of political occurrences. The European Refidents at all the Courts of the native Princes correfponded with him unremittedly. Copies of all thefe voluminous correfpon-dencies were neceffary for perpetual reference, and occa-fionally for authoritative infpection. The office therefore, wherein this bufinefs was managed, was actually and in-difpenfably "*required to enable the* Governor-General *to exe-* "*cute the duties of his ftation*," and confequently its expence a fair, juftifiable, and undeniable claim on the Company.

3. Houfe-

3. Houfe-rent for the Governor-General's Aids de Camp.

The Remarker has foftened fomewhat of his acrimony in only ftyling this charge *unbecoming* and *irregular*. He was aware that every fhadow of objection to the article might be done away in an inftant; yet rather than fay *nothing*, he was content to fay *nothing to the purpofe*.

The beft houfes in Calcutta will accommodate but very few inhabitants, and none of them are in any degree proportioned to the unavoidable fize of a Governor-General's family. It is true that Mr. Haftings *enjoyed a houfe both in town and country rent-free*, and that he held *another houfe in Calcutta at the Company's expence*. What then?— When the Company complimented their Governor-General with a houfe, did they mean to allow him nothing but fingle room for his own particular habitation? Did they mean that his military and private Secretaries, his Aids de Camp and Staff fhould lie in the open air, or hire houfes at their own expence? Did they mean that the Governor's Lady fhould have no private apartment to retire from the buftle, noife, and crowd of uninterrupted public bufinefs?—This indeed would have made the Governor fenfible that their " *mark of refpect* " was moft exclufively

clufively "*perfonal to him.*" But, to be ferious—it was certainly intended, that the houfe to be allowed to the Governor, fhould be fuch as could conveniently entertain all the neceffary appendages of his family. Had there been in Calcutta any one houfe large enough for the purpofe, Mr. Haftings *might,* and undoubtedly *would* have hired it at the Company's expence, whatever might have been the rent : and the only difference is, that he was obliged to have his refidence under three roofs inftead of one, to his own great inconvenience. It might as well be urged, that if the Governor-General had been fhut up in Fort William on the event of a fiege, he muft not have ventured to appropriate to himfelf and his fuite any greater portion of the barracks, than are allotted to the ordinary commander of the fort in time of peace. The number of thofe in employ near the Governor-General's perfon is, and *muft* be, the only meafure for the fize of his dwelling, and his houfe—rent muft be charged accordingly.

4. Diet and charges to Pundits—tranflating the Hindoo and Mahommedan Laws, and the expence of the Mahommedan Academy.

The

The very title of this account ſtamps and confirms the public nature of the charge.

For whom were theſe laws tranſlated?—For the public. Who gave authority to thoſe laws? The Company. Who obey them? The inhabitants of the Company's territories. Who diſpenſe them? Judges choſen from among the learned natives. Where might *they* acquire their learning? At the Academy.—Here then there appears *much* that concerns the Company, and *nothing* that concerns Mr. Haſtings.

The Mahommedan laws are the rule of right to all the Mahommedan inhabitants of Bengal. *Few* indeed compared to the Hindoos. But the Remarker is a better maſter of the ſubject than really to eſtimate them as only one in a hundred. Be that as it may, while the laws are *profeſſed* there muſt be *profeſſors.* The utility therefore of an academy, where thoſe laws may be taught, or where, at leaſt, a foundation may be laid for them, cannot be done away. In the poliſhed and permanent eſtabliſhments of European ſtates, the private foundations of individuals may preclude the neceſſity of public interference. Such foundations have in former ages flouriſhed in Indoſtan. For the pious abſurdity of atoning for a life of inceſſant

D   crimes

crimes by the foundation of a college or an hofpital has
not been confined to one climate or one religion. Weal-
thy guilt has of late been lefs repentant ; and the farcaftic
" Remarker allows with Mr. Haftings, " That the de-
" cayed remains [only] of thefe fchools are now to be
" feen in the principal cities of Indoftan."

There is no longer in Bengal the former fplendor of
its native Mahommedan court, nor the bait of lucrative of-
fices in the ftate to tempt men of ambition, on through the
toils and expences of a liberal education. Were there not a
feminary encouraged by public munificence, where learning might be acquired without much coft, and where the
profeffors of fcience might find an afylum at leaft, if not
a reward, in a few years the company's fubjects in
India would fink into the moft deplorable ftate of favage
and brutal ignorance.

In anfwer to the frivolous and flippant queftions, blurted
forth in the 28th page, it is fufficient to fay, that proofs
of the exiftence and utility of the inftitution can be fought
only on the fpot.—But, fays the Remarker, " *Who, in fhort,*
" *ever heard of his academy before ?*" I reply, *Thou art the*
man—For elfe, to a total want of every language of India
and a fupercilious difdain of all converfation with the mi-

ferable

ferable natives, muſt be added an utter ignorance of what paſſed at the Council Board in Calcutta, when the propriety of this eſtabliſhment was diſcuſſed—and that it was there both *diſcuſſed* and *admitted*, Mr. Haſtings has aſſerted in the letter before us.—After all, the academy is for natives, not Europeans—and the credit of the deſign, and the glory of its ſucceſs belong excluſively to Mr· Haſtings.—*He* has a heart calculated for the enjoyment of ſuch *moonſhine* gratifications. It follows to ſpeak of the expence——The article, " if proper (ſays the Remarker) " ought to have been provided for by the Board at Calcutta." Does he not know, and is it not *in proof* that the Board in granting its conſent *did ultimately provide for it?* " Af-
" ter a trial of about two years (See Mr. Haſtings's letter)
" finding that it (the academy) was likely to anſwer the
" end of its inſtitution, I recommended to the Board,
" and *obtained their conſent*, to paſs the ſubſequent expence
" of the eſtabliſhment to the account of the company,
" and to erect a building for the purpoſe, at my own im-
" mediate coſt, but for a company's *intereſt-note* granted
" me for the reimburſement of it."——The inſtitution therefore was ſolemnly, and authoritatively approved, and Mr Haſtings was permitted to advance the money out of his own pocket, at the uſual intereſt, for erecting the building.——What is there in this tranſaction to warrant

the

the Remarker's triumphant petulance ? Mr. Haftings never fought the oftentation of *paying* for the eftablifhment; he prided himfelf in commencing, fupporting, and compleating the defign. He firft liberally gave it a trial of two years at his own coft and charge. Had it *failed* we fhould have heard nothing of the demand, and Mr. Haftings muft have quietly fubmitted to the lofs. It is fingularly hard that he fhould be upbraided for it, when it did *not* fail, and when the Board, on the mature experience of his previous trial, chofe to encourage it. The Remarker then adds, " That he may have erected a building " for an academy is not unlikely, becaufe a building " fuppofes a contract ; and, *a contract makes the fortune of* " *a contractor.*" See what it is to be a calculator. The whole expence of maintaining Pundits during a long compilation of Hindoo laws, of tranflating the laws of Mahommed, fundry monthly falaries paid to fome of their moft learned profeffors, and other incidental matters—together with the charge for erecting the academy, amounts but to 85.357 Rupees—of which it may be fairly affumed, that 50000 Rupees is the utmoft coft of the edifice.——A contractor *make bis fortune* and build a college out of five thoufand pounds ! l

5. A Charge for Budgerows and Boats,

After a few defultory pages, we arrive at the remarks on this fifth article. Mr. Haftings fays, " His predecef- " fors always had an eftablifhment of this kind provided " for them," And, as the Remarker has not contradicted the affertion, it muft be true,——Are not boats fubject to decay? And muft not every eftablifhment of this kind be occafionally renewed?——" But (it feems) thefe boats are " fuperior in convenience and elegance to any that Mr. " Haftings has yet feen." What then? If the mechanic arts be improved in the country, it is a proof, that populalation, induftry and wealth have increafed at the fame time.——Is a convenient or elegant yacht incompatible with *fimplicity of manners?* Perhaps the Remarker would have advifed to buy up at auction one of the old city barges, and tranfport it to Bengal, in the room of a fhip's long-boat, for the ufe of the Governor-General.——But the Proprietors of India Stock are to hear with indignation, that their fervant's boats have been " *furnifhed with a* " *coft which would not be credited by thofe who have not feen* " *the fubjects of it.*" And what is this coft? 59,165 rup. including above two years wages to numerous crews of boatmen. Let but the Proprietors turn back to the charges

of

of boats, even for General Smith's deputation to Lucknow, they will find them to have exceeded 3 lacks of rupees.
"*The coſt, therefore, which would not be credited*" means
nothing more than that the Company have now, by Mr.
Haſtings's means, acquired an eſtabliſhment of boats more
convenient and more elegant than he had ever ſeen before,
at, comparatively, a hundredth part of the uſual expence—
A prodigious loſs, truly! and incurred too from a man
" in whoſe integrity the legiſlature have placed a diſtin-
" guiſhed confidence, and who, ſtanding high himſelf, is
" looked up to as an example,"

Boats are certainly " neceſſary to enable the Governor
" to execute the duties of his ſtation;" and therefore
Mr. Haſtings charged them to the Company.——The
amount, eſtimated at two years only, is but 2,465 rupees
a month—and the Company, at the end of this period, are
put into poſſeſſion of the beſt boats ever conſtructed in the
country, and nearly as good as new. And yet Mr.
Haſtings has condeſcended to apologize for having omitted
to lay their charge before the Board,

I am aſhamed to have dwelt ſo long upon ſo clear a
ſubject.

We

We come now to Mr. Haftings's private fortune. In page 37, the Remarker exults in exhibiting an amount of very nearly 34,000 pounds fterling, arranged under five heads only, of *little* articles gleaned from Mr. Haftings's paft expences. In page 40, he allows Mr. Haftings's whole domeftic expences to have been but 8,000 rupees a month. What is eafier than to fhew, that if thefe *little* articles of expence, gleaned out of paft accounts, amount (as by an average they are found to do) to about 2,335 rupees a month, it is impoffible that 8,000 rupees can be a fum large enough to entitle 2,335 rupees to the denomition of *little*. If, therefore, Mr. Haftings had expended but 8,000 rupees a month, for the fupport of his family, 2,335 rupees would never have fuggefted to his mind the idea of *little articles* gleaned from paft expences.——Mr. Haftings was not gaudy nor oftentatious—But his eftablifhment was magnificent, and his houfehold extenfive. It has been computed, that, one day with another, half a maund, or near 40 lb. of wax candles were confumed at his charge. This alone is an article of 1,200 rupees a month.

Mr. Haftings afferts, that his fortune is *fmall.*—The Remarker only proves, that it *might have been* large. His manners were fimple, and his drefs unaffected; and therefore, by the Remarker's fyftem, he had no fire in his kitchen, and hardly a glafs of wine to give to his guefts: Does he not know, that Mr. Haftings expended, and ultimately loft great fums in building? Were the coft and maintenance of all his horfes nothing? Did he never lend money, which he could not reafonably expect to recover? Or charitably give it away, without fo much as the form of an obligation for its return? Was he exempt from loffes, by remittances, or on refpondentia, or in any or all the means, by which the Remarker would have exhorted him to augment his fortune at fimple or compound intereft? Mr. Haftings never thought of infinuating that *he kept no accounts of his expenditure*; in the act of acknowledging that he has improvidently diffipated, or loft his allowances; yet the Remarker would infer the contrary. " it is true, fays he, (page 42) that he talks of his " inaccuracy, and would willingly be thought a man care- " lefs about money-matters : *But we have evidence to the* " *contrary before us.* He has kept an exact account of the " minuteft articles of expence, and even of his charities." Is it incompatible with extravagance to keep accounts? But becaufe Mr. Haftings *has kept accounts*, we have *evidence* (in the Remarker's language) that he has *not* been carelefs or inaccurate.——Had he no accountant—no clerk? Becaufe his money went too faft, was it therefor

difburfed

difburfed without a warrant ?—Timon's profufion was un-
limited, yet the faithful fteward had booked every item of
his liberalities.

" There is another way of eftimating his (Mr. Haft-
" ings's) fortune," fays the Remarker, " that is, if he were
" to be debited with the fums which he has been accufed
" of receiving.——In March, 1775, he was charged by
" the unfortunate Raja Nuncomar, with the receipt of
" various fums paid to him by the Raja to the amount
" of Sonaut Rupees 3,54,105, or about 36,000 l. The
" accufer not only fpecified all manner of particulars, but
" came forward, at every poffible perfonal. hazard,
" to make good his charge. If it was falfe, it was at
" once the moft daring and abfurd falfehood that ever
" was attempted. *Dolus in generalibus verfatur.* Falfe-
" hood never defcends to particulars. The Raja, how-
" ever, was inftantly hanged; and his charge, whether
" true or falfe, muft be difmiffed out of this account."
(Page 43.)

Falfe altogether——or where is it proved? were thefe
particulars ever publifhed, or were they known only
to the Members of the Council at that time? He
that runs may read the author's name here. *Monftretur
digitis Prætereuntium.* If the particulars of thefe bribes

E   had

had been ftated fo accurately, Nuncomar's death was by no means a fufficient reafon for their utter fuppreffion. neither he nor any other man of his rank in India, ever paid money with his own hands. Did he pay the fums in *Cafh* or *Bills?* In the one cafe he muft have had a *Dewan* or *Sircar*, in the other *a Banker*. Either or all of thefe might at leaft have been brought forward to authenticate the reality of the payments, though they might not be able to fpecify the confideration.——

But to calumnies of fuch impudent and flagrant noto-riety downright contradiction is the only anfwer.—It is *falfe* that Mr. Haftings ever received any money from Nuncomar. He detefted him, and never admitted him to the fmalleft fhare of his confidence. It is falfe that the Raja fpecified *all manner of particulars*, or *any* particu-lars: for if he had, there wanted not inclination nor in-duftry on the part of the majority at the Board to have profecuted the inveftigation, even with the *threads* and *remnants* of a particular.—It is *falfe* to affert that " *falfe-* " *hood never defcends to particulars:*" for a cafual or indifferent circumftance artfully thrown into a tale, is the moft obvious of all contrivances to make it pafs current; fo Falftaff could difcern *Kendal Green* upon three knaves, when it was fo dark, that he could not fee his own hand.

And

And this apothegm is moſt *ridiculouſly* as well as *falſely* applied to the charge exhibited by Nuncomar; for it is not likely that a man who was hanged on the fulleſt conviction for *one* forgery, ſhould be at all *delicate* in ſtringing together a number of plauſible particulars to give credibility to *another*. It is *falſe* that "the Raja was *inſtantly* "hanged" on preferring his falſe accuſation: for he was regularly tried and ſentenced according to law, and ſuffered to live much longer than uſual after condemnation. It is *falſe*, that his "charge (whether true or falſe) muſt "be diſmiſſed out of this account," in conſequence of the Raja's inſtant execution: for, if he had left behind him a circumſtantial account, with all manner of particulars, the dates of payment, the names of the perſons to whom paid, and by whom, and on what account, and the ſeveral ſums, would have afforded ample means for a compleat and deciſive diſcovery. This tale, therefore is *falſe in toto*, and *falſe in all its parts*, and I would ſtake my life that the Remarker himſelf does not believe one ſyllable of it.

If Nuncomar's *name* were not, by a kind of indefinable but obvious ſympathy, connected with *that* of our Remarker, *the aſſignment of the Maratta war to the account of Mr. Haſtings*, (page 38) would effectually have betrayed

the

the anonymous libeller.—" There live not three good men
" unhanged in England" who can affect to credit such
an abfurdity, " and one of them, God help the while,
" grows old ;" and has fcarcely travelled but in his clofet.
This affertion then is an after-birth to a ftill-born " Ad-
" drefs to the Proprietors of India Stock,"—*dated* from
" Calcutta the 1ft April, 1783"—but *fabricated* (like the
prefent trafh) within an hour's walk of Grub-ftreet.
Their common author, aware of his own maxim, " *Dolus*
" *in generalibus verfatur,*" has fprinkled each of them with
a variety of little local circumftances (as indeed he might
well do from experience), to increafe their plaufibility – for
" any artifice" as he unluckily blunders out in his 17th
page, " may deceive the multitude." He is welcome
however to this part of his charge un-refuted——I leave
him to make the moft of it.

To the laft but not the leaft of his fallacious infinuations
page 45 " He (Mr. Haftings) may have appropriated large
" fums to fervices not proper to be explained——He has
" wafted his fortune to obtain protection, and his poverty
" arifes from his fuccefs in corrupting the integrity of
" perfons whofe *truft* and *flation* gave them *power* to fupport
" him"—I anfwer that *no* falary, *no* emoluments would
have been fufficient to purchafe the variety of perfons who

4   have

have come into *truſt* and *ſtation* here during the period of Mr. Haſtings's Government: That he never was uniformly and vigorouſly ſupported by any one of the fleeting adminiſtrations, which have paſſed by him ;—That of thoſe adminiſtrations *one* was compoſed of the very men who then *did*, and who now *do*, ſtand forward with all the violence of inveterate enmity to accuſe him: and if he had attempted to corrupt them, or any one of them, while their " *truſt and ſtation gave them power to ſupport him*," they muſt be the greateſt *knaves* in the univerſe, if, after having contributed to impoveriſh him by accepting his bribes, they now move heaven and earth to undermine his honour and his life: or the greateſt *fools*, if, after having nobly rejected his dirty offers, they do not now in the true ſpirit of patriotiſm diſplay the iniquitous tranſaction to the world in all its foul detail of particulars.

P. S. A word or two of the falſe Engliſh attributed to Mr. Haſtings. The matter is indeed hardly worth notice; for a man's ſtyle may not be always equally pure : no imputation on the ſanity of his intellects notwithſtanding. But it ſhews the ingenuity of the Remarker in ſcrupulouſly making the moſt of all advantages. He has

however

however criticifed but *three* paffages; and in *two* of them
he is palpably wrong. They are

"Interefted note"

· "Profpects of futurity,"

And "difcharge viciffitudes."

The firft of thefe is a blunder made by the Remarker
himfelf, or his copyift; for in the original Letter, and in
the copy printed for the Houfe of Commons, the word is
intereft-note.—Technically, for a note bearing intereft.—
The Remarker firft fabricates the blunder, and then detects
it. "*Profpects of futurity*" is right; and the Remarker's ob-
fervation (page 32) is falfe and abfurd. Mr. Haftings
does *not* "call the latter part of his own life his Profpects
"of Futurity." But fays that "his profpects of futu-
"rity were unconnected with the view of his private
"concerns." A fchool-boy would have been flogged for
fo grofs a mifapplication. In the laft phrafe "difcharging
"the hard viciffitudes of his ftation"—there is certainly
an inconfiderable, but a very accountable deviation from
propriety of fpeech. Read the fentence as it ftands in the
Letter. Mr. Haftings had written "to difcharge the
"laborious duties;" and then, in the hurry of writing,
puts down the other member of his phrafe "hard vicif-
"fitudes;" omitting, and perhaps even thinking that he

had

had inferted the verb " *meet*," or whatever other word
might have occurred in the moment of compofition.
The fentence read with this infertion is perfectly pure—
" threatens me with a correfponding decay in whatever
" powers of mind I once poffeffed *to difcharge the laborious*
" *duties and* (meet) *the hard viciffitudes of my ftation.*"

T H E   E N D.

This Day is publifhed, Price 1s.

O B S E R V A T I O N S

O N   T H E

L A S T   D E B A T E

U P O N   T H E

DEHLY NEGOCIATIONS,

AND THE

PROPOSED IMPEACHMENT

O F

MR. HASTINGS.

Printed for JOHN STOCKDALE, oppofite Burlington-Houfe,
Piccadilly.

* 9 7 8 3 3 3 7 0 1 2 5 4 0 *